Christmas on the Porch

P. A. Oltrogge

WESTBOW
PRESS®
A DIVISION OF THOMAS NELSON
& ZONDERVAN

WestBow Press books may be ordered through booksellers or by contacting:

WestBow Press
A Division of Thomas Nelson & Zondervan
1663 Liberty Drive
Bloomington, IN 47403
www.westbowpress.com
1 (866) 928-1240

ISBN: 978-1-9736-4427-9 (sc)
ISBN: 978-1-9736-4426-2 (e)

Print information available on the last page.

WestBow Press rev. date: 11/07/2019

Contents

From the Author

Dear Friend,

It's my prayer that you will be blessed by the verses in this book—a Christmas blend, poetically penned.... Merry Christmas!

Sincerely,

P. A. Oltrogge

Christmas on the Porch

I stepped out onto the porch on a late, cold winter's night;
the snowfall was like glitter, casting sparkling light.

I tucked my scarf into my jacket to protect from the cold;
the moon and stars were out, shining brightly and bold.

I needed time away from thinking of Christmas preparations,
to take some time to think of He who was born for the nations.

A long time ago in Bethlehem, God sent us His only Son,
and filled the sky with angels to say that reconciliation had begun.

It was through the birth of Jesus and the life that He would live,
that all could find the Savior—Jesus would heal and would forgive.

Born in a lowly place, He exemplified a servant from the first
and would offer living water to quench any person's spiritual thirst.

He would follow the will of His Father in heaven, even to the cross.
There, His blood would be shed on Calvary so that no soul need be lost.

The temperature seemed to be dropping, so I needed to step back inside.
Let every heart prepare Him room, Christmas busyness being set aside.

> Joy to the world, the Lord is come!
> Let earth receive her King!
> Let every heart prepare Him room;
> and heaven and nature sing;
> and heaven and nature sing;
> and heaven, and heaven, and nature sing!

P. A. Oltrogge

A Message and Prayer from a Shepherd in the Field

I was out in the field with the other shepherds on what seemed like an ordinary night, when we suddenly were surrounded–by an extraordinary, glorious light.

I would never have thought to see an angel, but that's what I saw appear. He began to give us a message, saying, first, there was nothing to fear.

He continued, speaking of good tidings of great joy, for all people of the earth–for that day, in the city of David, had been Christ the Lord, the Savior's birth.

Then the angel spoke of a sign, which would help us to locate this wonder. He'd be wrapped in swaddling clothes, lying in a manger–then I heard what seemed like some thunder.

It turned out to be the sound of many angels–not just a few, but a multitude! They were praising God with great rejoicing, creating a festive mood.

"Glory to God in the highest, and on earth, peace, good will toward men!" These were the words they left us with, so we went on to Bethlehem then.

We were eager to follow the heavenly directive given to us that night; and just as the angel had specified, we found the Baby in a manger–God's "Light."

We stood in adoration of the Christ child, knowing His destiny was divine…and that He had been born to be our Savior–I knew then also that He was mine.

We thanked Mary and Joseph for this moment, having told them of the visitation in the field...then went on to make known to others the good news, that, to us, had been revealed.

What an amazing night I had experienced–the Lord visiting me in such a way! And may people of all future generations, receive this heralded Savior, I pray.

P. A. Oltrogge
(from the account in Luke 2)

"I have come as a light into the world, that whoever believes in Me should not abide in darkness." John 12:46 NKJV

"The people who walked in darkness have seen a great light; Those who dwelt in the land of the shadow of death, upon them a light has shined." Isaiah 9:2 NKJV

The Faith of Mary

Mary changed the course of this entire earth,
by accepting God's plan for the virgin birth.
Her agreement with the angel's words affirmed God's will,
and the words that she spoke are often quoted still.
She declared herself to be God's handmaid or servant;
in her, the Lord had found a heart that was fervent.
She had faith the Lord loved her and all of mankind;
she trusted in God's heart and not her own mind.
She was just a young woman of a tender age,
but she stepped out in faith onto the world's center stage.
Though startled at first by the angelic visitation,
her faith in God was strong enough to take up her station.
Likewise, it's wise today to ask the Lord to help us find
the plans and purposes for our lives that He has in mind.
By doing so, we ensure that we're on His sure quest,
for our loving Designer knows which plans are the best.
Jesus called His disciples to leave earthly pursuits
to follow Him and put down strong spiritual roots.
What He has for our lives can be discerned by His Word;
and through the power of the Holy Spirit, He also can be heard.
The more that we listen to Him, the more we obey,
the brighter the dawn grows to the full day.

P. A. Oltrogge

"But the path of the righteous is like the light of dawn, that shines brighter and brighter until the full day." Proverbs 4:18 NASB

"And in the sixth month, the angel, Gabriel, was sent from God unto a city of Galilee named Nazareth, to a virgin espoused to a man whose name was Joseph, of the house of David; and the virgin's name was Mary. And the angel came in unto her, and said, 'Hail, thou that art highly favored, the Lord is with thee: blessed art thou among women.' And when she saw him, she was troubled at his saying, and cast in her mind what manner of salutation this should be. And the angel said unto her, 'Fear not, Mary: for thou hast found favor with God.

"And, behold, thou shalt conceive in thy womb, and bring forth a son, and shalt call his name JESUS. He shall be great, and shall be called the Son of the Highest: and the Lord God shall give unto him the throne of his father David: And he shall reign over the house of Jacob forever; and of his kingdom there shall be no end.'

"Then said Mary unto the angel, 'How shall this be, seeing I know not a man?' And the angel answered and said unto her, 'The Holy Ghost shall come upon thee, and the power of the Highest shall overshadow thee: therefore also that holy thing which shall be born of thee shall be called the Son of God. And behold, thy cousin Elisabeth, she hath also conceived a son in her old age: and this is the sixth month with her, who was called barren. For with God nothing shall be impossible.'

"And Mary said, 'Behold the handmaid of the Lord; be it unto me according to thy word.' And the angel departed from her." Luke 1:26-38 KJV

Joseph's Example

Joseph, a son of David, took Mary for his wife,
believing she was carrying God's very sacred life.
Joseph stood by her when others may have condemned.
Joseph believed God when they didn't comprehend.

He was chosen by God, and it was to him that Mary and the Child
were sent. He became the protector of God's great intent.
Joseph was quick to recognize that in dreams God often spoke,
with messages from His angel, and he obeyed when he awoke.

Joseph named the baby, Jesus, just as he'd been told,
for He would save His people from sins, as said by the prophet of old.
In obedience, Joseph went to Egypt–"Out of Egypt did I call My Son."
Joseph had them stay until God said their time there was done.

We see him obeying God in Bible scene after scene.
Being warned of God, he went to Nazareth, so Jesus would be called a
Nazarene. His part was that of an earthly father, and he obeyed God in that
role. His heart to obey Him was needed to accomplish God's great goal.

Joseph's life seems an example of the importance of hearing and obeying
God's voice. Dear God, may I seek to do that in each and every choice.

P. A. Oltrogge

"…behold an angel of the Lord appeared to him in a dream, saying, 'Joseph,
son of David, do not be afraid to take Mary as your wife; for that which
has been conceived in her is of the Holy Spirit. And she will bear a Son;
and you shall call His name Jesus, for it is He who will save His people
from their sins.' Now all this took place that what was spoken by the
Lord through the prophet might be fulfilled, saying, 'BEHOLD, THE
VIRGIN SHALL BE WITH CHILD, AND SHALL BEAR A SON,
AND THEY SHALL CALL HIS NAME IMMANUEL,' which

translated means, 'God with us.' And Joseph arose from his sleep, and did as the angel of the Lord commanded him, and took her as his wife, and kept her a virgin until she gave birth to a Son; and he called His name Jesus." Matthew 1:20-25 NASB

(Further references in Matthew 2)

"Therefore the Lord Himself will give you a sign: Behold, a virgin will be with child and bear a son, and she will call His name Immanuel." Isaiah 7:14 NASB

"For a child will be born to us, a son will be given to us, And the government will rest on His shoulders; And His name will be called Wonderful Counselor, Mighty God, Eternal Father, Prince of Peace." Isaiah 9:6 NASB

Two Significant Births

The Hebrew people had prayed for a deliverer to be their long-promised King. While living under Roman rule, they looked for the answer that God would bring.

Then it came to pass that two little babies were born in the same time span. The lives of each one of them would be major in God's great redemptive plan.

One would be a prophet named John, the baptizer, and was the son of Zacharias, the priest. The other was Jesus, who would be the focus and celebration of God's greatest Passover Feast.

John's mother, Elizabeth, had longed for a child and rejoiced at the birth of her son. And Jesus' mother, Mary, told the angel who came that God's will for her should be done.

The angel, Gabriel, had first appeared to Zacharias and told him what to name his son...John, "The Lord is gracious," a preparer of the way for the Messiah, God's Anointed One.

When betrothed, Mary's Joseph had gained assurance from God, by having been visited in a dream too. Mary stayed with her cousin, Elizabeth, for a time before her own baby would become due.

These four parents realized, through faith, the significance of those entrusted to their care. A messenger of God, and Immanuel, "God With Us," were birthed in answer to prayer.

P. A. Oltrogge

(from Luke 1 and Matthew 1:18-25)

Written of Jesus:

"And the angel said unto her, 'Fear not, Mary: for thou hast found favour with God. And, behold, thou shalt conceive in thy womb, and bring forth a son, and shalt call his name JESUS. He shall be great, and shall be called the Son of the Highest, and the Lord God shall give unto him the throne of his father, David: And he shall reign over the house of Jacob for ever; and of his kingdom there shall be no end.' Then said Mary unto the angel, 'How shall this be, seeing I know not a man?' And the angel answered and said unto her, 'The Holy Ghost shall come upon thee, and the power of the Highest shall overshadow thee: therefore also that holy thing which shall be born of thee shall be called the Son of God. And behold, thy cousin Elisabeth, she hath also conceived a son in her old age: and this is the sixth month with her, who was called barren. For with God nothing shall be impossible.' And Mary said, 'Behold the handmaid of the Lord; be it unto me according to thy word.' And the angel departed from her." Luke 1:30-38 KJV

Written of John:

"And his father, Zacharias, was filled with the Holy Spirit, and prophesied, saying… 'And you, child, will be called the prophet of the Most High, for you will go on before the Lord to PREPARE HIS WAYS, to give to His people the knowledge of salvation by the forgiveness of their sins, because of the tender mercy of our God, with which the Sunrise from on high shall visit us, TO SHINE UPON THOSE WHO SIT IN DARKNESS AND THE SHADOW OF DEATH, to guide our feet into the way of peace.'" Luke 1:67 and 76-79 NASB

The Manger

Jesus…

It's a funny thing, but I never saw
Why You might have been laid in a bed of straw.
That's where the animals came to feed,
And that was representative of <u>our</u> daily need
Of the Bread of Life, which, Jesus, You are.
We're drawn to Your Word like wise men to a star.
To all people the angels proclaimed tidings of great joy,
By pointing to the birth of that God-indwelt boy,
Who lay down in the manger where the animals were fed.
Jesus–the Word was God–You're our daily bread.

P. A. Oltrogge

"In the beginning was the Word, and the Word was with God, and the Word was God." John 1:1 NASB

"Jesus said to them, 'I am the bread of life; he who comes to Me shall not hunger, and he who believes in Me shall never thirst.'" John 6:35 NASB

"And Joseph also went up from Galilee, from the city of Nazareth, to Judea, to the city of David, which is called Bethlehem, because he was of the house and family of David, in order to register, along with Mary, who was engaged to him, and was with child. And it came about that while they were there, the days were completed for her to give birth. And she gave birth to her first-born son; and she wrapped him in cloths, and laid Him in a manger, because there was no room for them in the inn."
Luke 2:4-7 NASB

Star Gazing Leads to the Star to be Praising

"... and behold, the star which they had seen in the East went before them, till it came and stood over where the young Child was. When they saw the star, they rejoiced with exceedingly great joy. And when they had come into the house, they saw the young Child with Mary His mother, and fell down and worshiped Him. And when they had opened their treasures, they presented gifts to Him: gold, frankincense, and myrrh. Matthew 2:9-11 NKJV

There's something very compelling about a brilliant star; and that, dear Lord, is what *You* are...

"The Bright and Morning Star," is one of Your titles, which inspires— "Glory to God in the highest" was sung at Your birth by heaven's angelic choirs.

The wise men followed the guiding light of a certain star in the sky, which led them to You, **the Bright and Morning Star— Jesus, the Son of the Most High.**

P. A. Oltrogge

"I, Jesus, have sent my angel to testify to you these things in the churches. I am the Root and the Offspring of David, the Bright and Morning Star." Revelation 22:16 NKJV

"And the angel said unto her, 'Fear not, Mary: for thou hast found favor with God. And, behold, thou shalt conceive in thy womb, and bring forth a son, and shalt call his name JESUS. He shall be great, **and shall be called the Son of the Highest:** and the Lord God shall give unto him the throne of his father David: And he shall reign over the house of Jacob forever; and of his kingdom there shall be no end." Luke 1:30-33 KJV

"For the Lord Most High is awesome; He is a great King over all the earth." Psalm 47:2 NKJV

"Offer to God thanksgiving, and pay your vows to the Most High." Psalm 50:14 NKJV

"He who dwells in the secret place of the Most High shall abide in the shadow of the Almighty." Psalm 91:1 NKJV

From the Biblical account in Matthew 2:1-12

Mary's, Elizabeth's, and Our Lord Jesus

Reference Luke 1:26-38

As foretold, Jesus was divinely conceived in the virgin Mary. Thereafter, she visited her cousin, Elizabeth, who was expecting a child, John, as well.

Upon arrival to her home, Mary greeted Elizabeth. Between the two, there must have been much to share and tell.

On hearing the greeting of Mary, Elizabeth felt the baby, who was already filled with the Holy Spirit, inside of her own womb leap for joy.

And then, by the Holy Spirit, Elizabeth spoke loudly, declaring that God's favor was great on Mary and her baby boy.

Elizabeth questioned why she was being granted such an honor, to be visited by Mary, "the mother of my Lord,"

but said that, through Mary, the world would have Jesus, the Savior—every believer's greatest reward.

The Song of Mary

"My soul magnifies the Lord, and my spirit has rejoiced in God my Savior. For He has regarded the lowly state of His maidservant; for behold, henceforth all generations will call me blessed. For He who is mighty has done great things for me, and Holy is His name. And His mercy is on those who fear Him from generation to generation.

"He has shown strength with His arm; He has scattered the proud in the imagination of their hearts. He has put down the mighty from their thrones, and exalted the lowly. He has filled the hungry with good things, and the rich He has sent away empty. He has helped His servant Israel, in remembrance of His mercy, as He spoke to our fathers, to Abraham and to his seed forever." Luke 1:46-55 NKJV

"And Mary remained with her about three months, and returned to her house." Luke 1:56 NKJV

The Perfect Gift

…A seasonal poem telling a story of a Christmastime visit—northern relatives visiting family in the southern U.S.…. They appreciate some brisk weather for a southern state as it reminds them of home. They shop for gifts and then take in an outdoor Christmas lighting display at a local church, where their attention turns to the most perfect gift of all.

A special time, pure white snowflakes,
Drifting down upon the roofs–
Moonlight reflecting on glistening snow blankets,
Years ago sleighs and horses hoofs…

Yet further south where palm trees stand,
It's not so cold this time of year.
But some nights can get brisk and that's all the better
To spread the feeling of Christmas cheer…

We've shopped for gifts
For this time of giving and receiving,
And have wrapped them quickly before they were seen.
Each one will be perfect, we're hoping, believing…

The bustle of shops seems far away,
And evening is calling us now to reflect
On a Gift long ago that was given to us
And was perfect in every respect…

It's time to take in a lighting display
On a pleasant walk in a peaceful church yard,
With cups of hot chocolate, wassail or cider
On a clear night that's moonlit and starred…

The tour begins with miniature train sets,
Captivating the children with their tiny village sites.
But all are in awe of the amazing task done
By those who had strung high the Christmas tree lights...

Tones and bells, soft, then louder;
Carolers round the bend–they're rightly bringing
The message of what it is all about–
The birth of our Savior is why they're singing...

Bethlehem, the manger, shepherds and wise men–
The Nativity glows, reminding us of these;
But mostly the Lord, Jesus Christ, we think on–
So grateful He came, we're down on our knees....

Oh hear the angel voices! Oh night divine! Oh night when Christ was born!

P. A. Oltrogge

Have You "Seen" Jesus?

In Jerusalem, there was a devout man named Simeon, back in New Testament days, who'd been waiting for the promised Messiah, in order to give Him praise.

The Holy Spirit was upon Simeon and had revealed that he wouldn't die until he would get to see that One, who was the object of his heart's cry.

One day the Spirit led him to the Temple and there he saw a child, whom he knew, by the Spirit's prompting, to be the One born undefiled.

Mary and Joseph were amazed to hear what Simeon then said about their boy. Jesus would cause many in Israel to fall, but to many others He would bring joy.

Simeon warned that many would oppose Him–the deepest thoughts of hearts would be revealed. A sword would pierce Mary's very soul– a reference to the cross, to which He'd yield.

Simeon said Jesus was sent as a sign from God, to reveal Himself and be a light...to every nation upon the earth. "The glory of God's people Israel" was His birthright.

Just as Simeon was speaking with Mary and Joseph, another given to prophecy came by–Anna, who never left the temple, but stayed day and night, raised her praises high.

How about you? Have you "seen" the Savior, as these people did who were old? Assurance and peace was theirs, having seen Jesus, whose life became the greatest story ever told!

P. A. Oltrogge

"Now Lord, Thou dost let Thy bond-servant depart in peace, according to Thy word; For my eyes have seen Thy salvation, Which Thou hast prepared in the presence of all peoples, A LIGHT OF REVELATION TO THE GENTILES, and the glory of Thy people Israel."
Luke 2:29-32 NASB

(Luke 2:21-38 for the entire account of Simeon and Anna)

Emmanuel, God With Us

Emmanuel, God with us…
You see, we are not alone.
Emmanuel, God with us…
Through the birth of a Child, God's presence was shown.
He couldn't leave us without knowledge of His love,
But made Himself known, coming down from above.
Emmanuel, God with us…
From God, the Father, came a Baby so mild.
Emmanuel, God with us…
God's Son was embodied in a holy Child.
Born of a virgin, the handmaiden of the Lord–
From His life, the goodness of God would be poured.
After humble beginnings in a manger stall,
His Name would become great–He would die for all,
So that any individual living on this earth
Could personally know their God of great worth.
Emmanuel, God with us…
It's the greatest Name known.
Emmanuel, God with us…in Jesus…
And now we need never be alone!

P. A. Oltrogge

"In that day you shall know that I am in My Father, and you in Me, and I in you." John 14:20 NASB

"And Jesus came up and spoke to them, saying, 'All authority has been given to Me in heaven and on earth. Go therefore and make disciples of all the nations, baptizing them in the name of the Father and the Son and the Holy Spirit, teaching them to observe all that I commanded you; and lo, I am with you always, even to the end of the age.'" Matthew 28:18-20 NASB

Foretold and Fulfilled

Prophecies and fulfillment (Old and New Testaments) on the birth and life of Jesus Christ

In (Genesis 12:3 and 22:18) the Lord told Abraham that by His design, the blessing of the Messiah would come from his (Abraham's) own line. (Matthew 1:1)

The Messiah's mother would be a virgin–Immanuel, He'd be called. (Isaiah 7:14) By an angel in a dream, to Joseph, this was confirmed and recalled. (Matthew 1:18-23)

(Genesis 17:19 and Numbers 24:17) reference Isaac and Jacob, these two– (Matthew 1:2, 16) shows Jesus Christ as a descendent of theirs, so this became true.

(Micah 5:2) prophesies Bethlehem Ephrathah as the town of Jesus' birth. (Luke 2:1-7) tells how that came about, making it a place of special worth.

In (Hosea 11:1) is the prophetic, "Out of Egypt, I called My Son." In (Matthew 2:13-15) an angel warned Joseph to take Mary and the Child to Egypt, to protect God's Holy One.

He would be a member of the tribe of Judah, as recorded in (Genesis 49:10)– In (Luke 3:33) it's confirmed, in the genealogy of Jesus, how that had actually been.

Some see, as prophetic, Jesus entering the temple noted in (Malachi 3:1). Then in (Luke 2:25-33), we see Mary and Joseph bringing into the temple their son.

(Jeremiah 23:5) The Lord said He would raise up for David a righteous Branch–a King to reign. In (Matthew 1:6), that the Messiah would come from the house of David is again made plain.

Great sorrow is predicted in (Jeremiah 31:15) to come at the time of the Messiah's birth. Herod kills boys two and under, causing mothers to grieve at their children's irreplaceable worth. (Matthew 2:16-18)

Jesus' life, death, resurrection, ascension, and seating at God's right hand: (Psalm 22:16; Psalm 16:10; Isaiah 53:10-11; Psalm 68:18; Psalm 110:1) Shown to be fulfilled, as God had planned: (1 Peter 2:21-22; Luke 23:33; Acts 2:25-32, Acts 1:9; Hebrews 1:3)

P. A. Oltrogge

"And she gave birth to her first-born son, and she wrapped Him in cloths, and laid Him in a manger, because there was no room for them in the inn."
Luke 2:7 NASB

Keeping Christmas Every Day

It's a good thing that we're reminded of the famous old
Charles Dickens tale of a man named Ebenezer Scrooge and a life
that had almost failed...

to embrace all of the kindness and compassion that could be spread around.
Instead, Ebenezer's greed and selfishness caused his life to be sadly bound.

The "ghost" of an old business partner appeared to him one Christmas Eve—
and told him he'd be visited by "spirits," who'd have insights for him to
receive.

If they could have him look back and remember some things that had
been good—then see in the present and the future the things that he really
should,

then his life might still be rescued from a bankruptcy of the soul...
So, as each Christmas spirit visited in the night, that was their
intended goal.

He'd just arrived at home, with resentment of paying Bob Cratchit,
his clerk, for the next day, Christmas Day, since Bob wouldn't even
have to work.

His nephew, Fred, had arrived that day with a cheerful "Merry
Christmas" greeting. "Bah, humbug," was Ebenezer's reply, as usual,
at this time of their meeting.

Fred's invitation to Christmas dinner, he also had declined once again,
and refused a plea by men who'd asked if he could help others not as
fortunate as him.

So, one by one, the spirits awoke him, taking him first on a journey to recall when he was a young apprentice to Mr. Fezziwig, who was generous and kind to all.

He saw his fiancee, Belle, who'd walked away due to realizing his first love was the pursuit of money and success, which he couldn't seem to put her above.

Perhaps, seeing his early childhood, too, when he had experienced love's neglect, made him start to rethink his own neglect of others, who needed attention and respect.

The spirit of Christmas present brought him to Bob Cratchit's family holiday– where, despite being poor, they were thankful to God and always took time to pray.

He learned of their sweet child, Tiny Tim, who needed medical care beyond their means. This began to touch Ebenezer's soul, at last, to see such a heart-wrenching scene.

He saw the celebration at Fred's house, where friends were mocking Ebenezer's inability to share. But Fred only spoke kind words of pity for his Uncle–his love for him was always there.

The spirit of the present revealed children, Ignorance and Want, shivering beneath its robe, representing the less fortunate whom we're to help and are with us throughout the globe.

The ghost of Christmas yet to come revealed funerals, one of a man who no one mourned. Then Ebenezer also saw the Cratchit home, where Tiny Tim had died–the family there, forlorn.

He ultimately learns that the man not mourned was himself, to his great shock and dismay. He begs the spirit to give him another chance to make amends–then he awakes to Christmas Day.

Immediately, Scrooge sends the Crachits a huge turkey, which was, to them, a gift that was profuse. Next, he encounters those who had asked of his donation–his wallet now was generous and loose.

Then, on to Fred's house, the changed Ebenezer proceeds, to inquire if he could still join them... to celebrate God's goodness at Christmas and always! This story is truly a meaningful gem.

P. A. Oltrogge

(The above synopsis from *A Christmas Carol* by Charles Dickens)

(In reality, the spirit world consists of God and His angels, the devil and evil spirits. But the theme of the story about the Christian love we're to share is certainly true and Biblical.)

An Old-Fashioned Christmas

May you experience an old-fashioned Christmas these days.
If you live where there's snow, some rent and ride sleighs
to enjoy the jingling of harness bells as the horses clomp along—
then head home for hot chocolate…or spiced cider that's strong.

Perhaps you'll find some old-fashioned gifts under the tree.
Something homemade by a loved one is a cherished specialty.
And for those who are talented, being musically blessed,
bring out your instruments for Christmas caroling with the rest.

Even planning an old-fashioned, door-to-door caroling party
is a great way to share Jesus' birth, with voices so hearty!
Back home for old-fashioned recipes, a fireplace's welcome glow…
then on to a Christmas Eve church service where more joy will flow!

If a church has an organ, its deep tones can exemplify
the deep love of God, greater than any gift one can buy.
For God sent His Son…a "God-fashioned," true story,
and so up-to-date. He's still our Savior from Glory!

P. A. Oltrogge

"And Mary said, 'My soul magnifies the Lord, and my spirit has rejoiced in God my Savior.'" Luke 1:46-47 NKJV

"But when the fullness of the time had come, God sent forth His Son, born of a woman, born under the law, to redeem those who were under the law, that we might receive the adoption as sons.

"And because you are sons, God has sent forth the Spirit of His Son into your hearts, crying out, 'Abba, Father!'" Galatians 4:4-6 NKJV

"...that Christ may dwell in your hearts through faith; that you, being rooted and grounded in love, may be able to comprehend with all the saints what is the width and length and depth and height—to know the love of Christ which passes knowledge; that you may be filled with all the fullness of God." Ephesians 3:17-19 NKJV

Nighttime Snowfall

In many regions, Christmas often comes with snow...

To this day, I love to watch the snow falling, so very peacefully at night, descending softly and serenely, glistening in the moonlight.

I remember, as children, wintry evenings, when the winds would blow... heading down our long, country driveway, to help our father shovel snow.

We sensed the peace of the Lord outside amid the drifts so deep, and laughed together, as we worked, before heading inside for the night to sleep.

P. A. Oltrogge

"Have you entered the treasury of snow...?" Job 38:22

"He gives snow like wool...." Psalm 147:16

"Peace I leave with you; My peace I give to you; not as the world gives do I give to you. Let not your heart be troubled, neither let it be afraid." *Words of Jesus* in John 14:27

Scriptures NKJV

The Heart of Christmas

For God so loved the world...
Can we comprehend His very big heart?
All the way back to Adam and Eve,
He loved us from the start.

God, the Father, would send a Savior
through Jesus Christ, His Son.
Born of the virgin, Mary--
through Jesus, His plans would be done.

Jesus, the Son, would die for our sins;
He would teach us about loving and giving.
I thank God for the gift of Jesus at Christmas,
who renews my faith always for living.

P. A. Oltrogge

"For God so loved the world that He gave His only begotten Son, that whoever believes in Him should not perish but have everlasting life." John 3:16 NKJV

"I have come that they may have life, and that they may have it more abundantly." John 10:10 NKJV

"May the Lord direct your hearts into the love of God and into the steadfastness of Christ." 2 Thessalonians 3:5 NASB

"A new commandment I give to you, that you love one another, even as I have loved you." John 13:34 NASB

"All the paths of the Lord are lovingkindness and truth to those who keep His covenant and His testimonies." Psalm 25:10 NASB

Never a Blue Christmas

A dimly lit stable or cave on that long-ago, destined night,
suddenly became a hallowed place, because of the newly arrived "Light."

Animals were resting nearby as the baby took His first breath.
He was sent from heaven to deliver this world from the snare of sin
and death.

Shepherds watching their flock by night were amazed by an angelic
visitation–telling them a Savior had been born–Christ the Lord, for
people of every nation.

"Glory to God in the highest, and on earth peace, good will toward men,"
was further proclaimed by a multitude of angels on what had taken
place then.

Straightway the shepherds went to Bethlehem to worship the baby in the
stall–the One who'd been sent to live among mankind but would give His
life for us all.

Death on a criminal's cross, followed by victorious resurrection, were
in the future of this newborn child, who would live a life of perfection.

If anything has gotten you down today, and at Christmas you're feeling
blue, just remember that all of the love God has still shines through Jesus...
for you.

P. A. Oltrogge

"Glory to God in the highest, and on earth peace, good will toward men."
Luke 2:14 KJV

"In Him was life, and the life was the light of men." John 1:4 NKJV

"Again therefore Jesus spoke to them, saying, 'I am the light of the world;
he who follows Me shall not walk in the darkness but shall have the light
of life." John 8:12 NASB

Cherished "Christmas of My Childhood" Memories

We always met at our grade school on an often snowy Christmas Eve, anticipating the gifts back home that we knew we would receive.

But thoughts, really, were on the Lord Jesus and the amazing story that we would be telling of God sending us His Son amidst angelic glory.

We each had a part we had practiced for the yearly Christmas Eve service— those who may have had a bigger role were sometimes a little bit nervous.

The atmosphere was one of warmth, though, but so respectful of the divine— at my church very many years ago, these Christmas memories of mine.

We stepped outside the school and crossed over the connecting street to the large decorated church sanctuary where everyone would meet.

To us children, the lights and nativity were always greatly impressive. Beautifully-ornamented, tall Christmas trees made the night so festive.

Boys wearing new suits and ties and the girls in fine dresses sewn began to sing the great Christmas carols, backed by the organ's deep tone.

Often a solo was sung—one of the most endearing was "O Holy Night," which spoke of the guiding star and its sweetly gleaming light.

This song told of the wise men who came from a distant Orient land, and how we were meant to love each other, as God had always planned.

"The weary world rejoices" were words that carol would recall, and that Jesus Christ had been born to us in a lowly manger stall.

"His law is love and His gospel is peace." I remember the song so well, along with the serenity felt, as we heard the old church steeple bell.

Some of the children had the roles of shepherds or of the wise men to play. Of course, there were Mary and Joseph by the Baby in the hay.

We were depicting the humble place where that great King had arrived– the Giver of everything good in life that could ever be wanted or derived.

"Joy to the World" was sung with robust joy to the pipe organ music's final beats, after which we returned to our classrooms for sacks of nuts and other treats.

Heading home in the car with our families to continue the Christmas Eve fest, we knew it was because of Jesus, that our lives were truly blessed.

Perhaps this reminds of your own childhood. If not, come now to join in its peace. God wants you in His family forever, to abide in His love that will never cease.

P. A. Oltrogge

O Holy Night

O holy night, the stars are brightly shining.
It is the night of our dear Savior's birth.
Long lay the world in sin and error pining,
'til He appeared and the soul felt its worth.
A thrill of hope, the weary world rejoices,
for yonder breaks a new and glorious morn.

Fall on your knees, O hear the angel voices,
O night divine, O night when Christ was born,
O night divine, O night, O night divine.

Led by the light of Faith serenely beaming,
with glowing hearts by His cradle we stand.
So led by light of a star sweetly gleaming,
here came the wise men from Orient land.
The King of Kings lay thus in lowly manger;
in all our trials, born to be our friend.

He knows our need, to our weakness is no stranger;
Behold your King! Before Him lowly bend!
Behold your King! Before Him lowly bend!

Truly He taught us to love one another;
His law is love and His gospel is peace.
Chains shall He break, for the slave is our brother;
and in His Name, all oppression shall cease.
Sweet hymns of joy in grateful chorus raise we;
let all within us praise His holy Name.

Christ is the Lord! O praise His Name forever;
His power and glory evermore proclaim.
O night divine, O night, O night divine!

*(music by Adolphe Adam
words by Placide Cappeau)*

On an Evening Walk Outside of Bethlehem

I was taking an evening walk, when I saw some shepherds in a field.
Then I saw a light surround them—they trembled, their fear revealed.

The light grew brighter, and it became an even more glorious light.
Then I realized that we were all seeing an angel on that night.

He came and stood before the shepherds—I was able to hear him some...
something about there being good news and that a Savior had come.

Next, to my absolute amazement, suddenly the night sky was filled
with what looked like an army of angels—a scene with which I was thrilled!

They shared a message of peace on earth, with their voices raised,
proclaiming now good will toward men and that God be praised!

They greatly were rejoicing, but then suddenly disappeared from sight.
Later, in town, the shepherds confirmed to me all that I'd seen that night.

They said they'd gone on, as well, to locate the One of whom they were
told...just a newborn baby in a manger, but the divine Child for them to
behold!

P.A. Oltrogge

"And suddenly there was with the angel a multitude of the heavenly host
praising God, and saying. 'Glory to God in the highest, and on earth peace,
good will toward men.'" Luke 2:13-14 KJV

"Suddenly, the angel was joined by a vast host of others—the armies of
heaven—praising God and saying 'Glory to God in highest heaven, and
peace on earth to those with whom God is pleased.'" Luke 2:13-14 NLT

Like a Shepherd

"Like a shepherd He will tend His flock,
In His arm He will gather the lambs,
And carry them in His bosom;
He will gently lead the nursing ewes."

Isaiah 40:11 NASB

————————————————————————

While shepherds watched their flocks by night,
An angel appeared, and God's glory shone bright.
The angel told the shepherds to not be afraid
Since a proclamation of great joy was being made!
A Savior for all people was born, who was Christ the Lord!
And then more angels praised God for the Baby adored.
Straightway to Bethlehem the shepherds went
To see this One Whom God had sent.
To everyone they saw, they made known what was told
Of God's gift, Who was cut from the shepherd's mold.
He would have a flock–the Good Shepherd He would be.
He would die for that flock, both for you and for me.
To rescue and die for the lambs–no greater love
Could have been sent to us from above.
If you're not yet His lamb, be aware there is danger–
We have need of the Good Shepherd, once a babe in a manger.
Just receive Him as Savior–then learn of His great care
In shepherding your life as you come to Him in prayer.
At Christ's birth, we were blessed, and God's message came then—
Of "peace on earth and good will toward men!"

P. A. Oltrogge

"But as many as received Him, to them He gave the right to become children of God, even to those who believe in His name, who were born not of blood, nor of the will of the flesh, nor of the will of man, but of God." John 1:12 NASB

"I am the door; if anyone enters through Me, he shall be saved, and shall go in and out, and find pasture. The thief comes only to steal, and kill, and destroy: I came that they might have life and might have it abundantly. I am the Good Shepherd; the Good Shepherd lays down His life for the sheep." John 10:9-11NASB

"Glory to God in the highest, and on earth peace, good will toward men." Luke 2:14 KJV

The Innkeeper

"And it came to pass in those days that a decree went out from Caesar Augustus that all the world should be registered. This census first took place while Quirinius was governing Syria. So all went to be registered, everyone to his own city.

"Joseph also went up from Galilee, out of the city of Nazareth, into Judea, to the city of David, which is called Bethlehem, because he was of the house and lineage of David, to be registered with Mary, his betrothed wife, who was with child." Luke 2:1-5 NKJV

———————————————————

A couple stopped at our Bethlehem inn, having come from quite a distance away. But due to the census, I had no rooms left at all in which any more people could stay.

The husband declared that his wife was ready, at any moment, to give birth. So I thought of the stable to offer them, hoping it might be of, at least, some worth.

There just was something about them, and my wife had sensed it, too. But because of the incoming crowds that day, there was nothing else we could do.

My wife took over some swaddling cloths and things she'd kept for a baby's birth. She overheard the soon-to-be parents speak of their expected child's great worth.

Later, in the inn, we thought that we heard the sound of a baby's cry... That evening, we saw a group of shepherds there, who, for some reason, had stopped by.

We finally got some rest for the night–the inn was full with those who'd traveled far; and I turned and looked out the window, where I saw the most brilliant star….

It's said you can entertain angels, without being fully aware… So I wondered if Someone greater than angels was connected with that special couple there.

P. A. Oltrogge

"And she brought forth her firstborn Son, and wrapped Him in swaddling cloths, and laid Him in a manger, because there was no room for them in the inn." Luke 2:7 NKJV

Yours Is a Wonderful Life

If your world seems to be in turmoil, and you're experiencing trouble or strife, it would be beneficial to remember the Christmas tale, "It's a Wonderful Life!"

Is there a "Mr. Potter" in your days, who has been greedy and domineering, while you've been working hard to do what's right...and to be God-fearing?

If things have come to a head, and you think there's no way through, remember how the angel, Clarence, showed George Bailey a thing or two.

George had to rescue him from drowning, which took his mind off his own woes. Then Clarence "showed" him Bedford Falls, if it hadn't had him to fight its foes.

Instead of a family-friendly town, it had become degraded, far below...the standard of a great place to live, through which good things could flow.

And the people who were important to him had lives that weren't complete, simply because he hadn't been there in Bedford Falls for them to meet.

At the end of the visitation by the angel, George realized the joy of just being alive. Likewise, we've got God and the angels despite problems with which we strive.

George's friends came through, as well, with appreciation for things he'd done. As the Bible says, God will complete the work in us that He's already begun.

P. A. Oltrogge

"I thank my God upon every remembrance of you, always in every prayer of mine making request for you all with joy, for your fellowship in the gospel from the first day until now, being confident of this very thing, that He who has begun a good work in you will complete it until the day of Jesus Christ." Philippians 1:3-6 NKJV

"The thief does not come except to steal, and to kill, and to destroy. I have come that they may have life, and that they may have it more abundantly." John 10:10 NKJV

"Are they (the angels) not all ministering spirits sent forth to minister for those who will inherit salvation?" Hebrews 1:14 NKJV

"He who dwells in the secret place of the Most High shall abide under the shadow of the Almighty. I will say of the Lord, 'He is my refuge and my fortress; my God, in Him I will trust.'" Psalm 91:1-2 NKJV

Children Love to Sing of the Newborn King

"And the Word became flesh and dwelt among us, and we beheld His glory, the glory as of the only begotten of the Father, full of grace and truth." John 1:14 NKJV

If there had never been a Savior, Christmas carols would never have been heard. We wouldn't have learned that the baby in the manger was God's very Word.

If there had never been that baby's birth, then when each December comes around, we wouldn't sing of "Joy to the World," but merely of some snowfall on the ground.

Songs of snowmen or of reindeer can't bless young children like songs that show–that they've a God of love, who created the real, live reindeer and the snow.

"Away in a manger, no crib for His bed, the little Lord Jesus laid down his sweet head; the stars in the sky look down where He lay" are words that bless so much more instead.

"The little Lord Jesus asleep on the hay" helps children to understand Christmas Day. "Oh Little Town of Bethlehem," song of His birthplace, has words that anyone can pray.

On a silent, holy night, all was calm and all was bright, when a virgin gave birth–to a holy infant, tender and mild. A child senses peace by this carol on Jesus' worth.

When children know of God's gift of the Savior, they're blessed to have the realization that lighted trees and giving of gifts are in honor of the Son of God's birthday celebration!

P. A. Oltrogge

O Little Town of Bethlehem

Oh, little town of Bethlehem,
how still we see thee lie.
Above thy deep and dreamless
sleep, the silent stars go by.
Yet in thy dark streets shineth,
the everlasting light.
The hopes and fears of all
the years are met in thee tonight.

For Christ is born of Mary
and gathered all above;
while mortals sleep,
the angels keep
their watch of wondering love.
Oh, morning stars together
proclaim the Holy birth.
And praises sing
to God the King,
and peace to men on earth.

How silently, how silently
the wondrous gift is given.
So God imparts to human hearts
the blessings of His heaven.
No ear may hear His coming,
but in this world of sin,
where meek souls
will receive Him still,
the dear Christ enters in.

Oh, holy child of Bethlehem
descend to us we pray.
Cast out our sin and enter in,
be born in us today.
We hear the Christmas angels
the great, glad tidings tell.
Oh come to us, abide with us,
our Lord, Emmanuel!

(Words by Phillips Brooks

Music by Lewis H.Redner)

Christ, Carols, and Cookies

At Christmastime, in my old country home, a much anticipated day… was the day on which we made cookies in a traditional, old-fashioned way.

An old family recipe for Christmas hard cookies was always the trusted guide, while carols played on the record player, and, often, snow was falling outside.

Those cookies, to this day, are favorites, though some joke about them being too hard…enough to use them for traction under car tires, if there's ice out in the yard!

But that joke was really a myth, which by tasting, could easily be debunked. But, if preferred, there was always fresh coffee into which the cookies could be dunked!

Rolling them out to just the right thinness, yet making sure they wouldn't be wrinkled…was an important job, as well as the jobs of cutting them out and seeing that they were sprinkled.

Red and green sugars or candied, tiny beads were applied to angels, bells, and stars. Once cooled off from having been baked in the oven, they were packed away in tins or glass jars.

Mother, grandmother, and children were busy with the project for quite long. Some of the "workers" left for the piano to play a favorite Christmas song.

All of this was done in anticipation of Christmas Eve and the following Day, when we would be celebrating the birth of Christ, who Mary had placed in a manger on some hay.

Yes, those cookie bells spoke of ringing out the message of the Savior's birth. The star cookies reminded of the famous star that led the wise men to the King of heaven and earth.

The angel cookies depicted the angelic hosts which rejoiced on that holy night…when shepherds were amazed to hear of the good news, despite their initial fright.

On cookie-baking day, it didn't need to be dark to turn on the lights of the tree. It was a grand time to celebrate the Light of the World, who came and still shines today and for all eternity.

P. A. Oltrogge

"...The light shines in the darkness, and the darkness can never extinguish it." from John 1:5 NLT

Choosing the Real Versus the Artificial

I remember many chilly Christmases past, as you likely do as well… going to a local tree lot, to choose the best tree, as far as we could tell.

Some may have been too short, and some may have been too tall; then, finally, we would discover…the best one for us of them all.

At some point, years ago, it became popular to switch to an artificial pine, but they never truly could satisfy this old-fashioned heart of mine.

When it comes to choosing the truth about God, there really is only one way. Jesus—the way, the truth, and the life, who came to us, first, as a baby on the hay.

You can't make up your own version of God—an artificial "god" won't do. For God so loved the world that He sent His only Son…this He did for you.

So as you go about enjoying the beautiful trees of the Christmas season, remember God's Biblical and satisfying truth—that Jesus IS its reason.

Most trees are topped by an angel or a star, reminding us of Christ's birth. Rejoice, for God loves you very much; and Jesus is (the real) Lord of heaven and earth!

P. A. Oltrogge

"Jesus saith unto him, 'I am the way, the truth, and the life: no man cometh unto the Father, but by me.'" John 14:6 KJV

"For God so loved the world, that he gave his only begotten Son, that whosoever believeth in him shall not perish, but have everlasting life." John 3:16 KJV

"May you experience the love of Christ, though it is too great to understand fully. Then you will be made complete with all the fullness of life and power that comes from God." Ephesians 3:19 NLT

Christmas is...

Christmas is all about God becoming Man, by a birth that was heaven-sent. The birth of mankind's Savior is what Christmas has always meant.

Jesus Christ, God's holy infant, slept in a stable on a bed of hay, which demonstrated that genuine humility is always the Lord's way.

This newborn baby would grow up to be the greatest teacher of all time. It's of His life and redemptive work that the joyous Christmas bells chime.

Mary and Joseph were chosen as parents to nurture God's very own Son— to guard and protect Him carefully until their guidance over Him was done.

Then Jesus began to follow what His Heavenly Father was conveying— and His Father's will was reflected in the things He began doing and saying.

He taught by Word and example, but eventually was led to a hill, where something more lowly than His birth in a stable was awaiting Him still.

From the stable to a criminal's cross, the Spirit of God was His guide. Christmas is Christ—He was born for us all, and for all of us He died.

But a joyous resurrection came about—He'd vanquished all of His foes! Now, we, too, can walk in newness of life because Jesus Christ arose.

The little town of Bethlehem is where Christ's ministry began... Foretold and fulfilled, Christ accomplished for us God's redemptive plan.

So share, "A blessed Merry Christmas!" greeting, honoring the Biblical scene... of the beautiful Nativity of Christ, something "Happy Holidays" can never mean.

P. A. Oltrogge

But as many as received him, to them gave he power to become the sons of God, even to them that believe on his name." John 1:12 KJV

A Star for the Magi, a Star for Us

"...they went their way, and lo, the star, which they had seen in the east, went before them, until it came and stood over where the Child was. And when they saw the star, they rejoiced exceedingly with great joy. And they came into the house and saw the Child with Mary His Mother; and they fell down and worshiped Him; and opening their treasures they presented to Him gifts of gold and frankincense and myrrh." Matthew 2:9-11 NASB

The Bible relates that some magi sought
a gift so priceless that it couldn't be bought.
A star was their guide in this long-ago quest;
and it went before them, coming to rest,
over the place where God decreed it should,
designating the Christ child—and there it stood.
It must have been brilliant as it stopped above
to point out the gift of God's divine love.
They worshiped Jesus there, going inside,
trusting that the star was their heaven-sent guide.
The child was the very reason God had brought them to this place,
and they sensed that redemption was theirs to embrace.
A Redeemer God had sent, as had been foretold—
The magi presented gifts—myrrh, frankincense, and gold.
God's righteousness and holiness would require a sacrifice—
that justice would be met when this Child paid the price.
He would live a perfect life, fulfilling all that's right,
and would urge all to repentance, saying He was the world's Light.
As an individual, you may think that your life has been good—
but "falling short of God's glory" needs to be understood.
God sent for all a Savior, an old familiar story—
only Christ's sinless life met and satisfied that glory.
Fitting it was for a sparkling star's light
to magnify the greatest Light on that special night.

Today God sends His Spirit to lead and be *your* guide—
It's standing above the Lord's house, inviting you to come inside.
There find the God-sent Christ for you to worship and believe.
You'll find that He gives gifts to *you*—from His goodness you'll receive!

P. A. Oltrogge

"Again therefore Jesus spoke to them, saying, 'I am the light of the world, he who follows Me shall not walk in the darkness, but shall have the light of life.'" John 8:12 NASB

"But now apart from the Law, the righteousness of God has been manifested, being witnessed by the Law and the Prophets, even the righteousness of God through faith in Jesus Christ for all those who believe, for there is no distinction; for all have sinned and fall short of the glory of God, being justified as a gift by His grace through the redemption which is in Christ Jesus; whom God displayed publicly as a propitiation in His blood through faith. This was to demonstrate His righteousness because in the forbearance of God, He passed over the sins previously committed, for the demonstration, I say, of His righteousness at the present time, that He might be just and the justifier of the one who has faith in Jesus."
Romans 3:21-26 NASB

"Every good thing bestowed and every perfect gift is from above, coming down from the Father of lights, with whom there is no variation or shifting shadow." James 1:17 NASB

The Nativity, God's Prime "Ornament"

Old, familiar ornaments for our evergreen…and bright, new ornaments we've not yet seen–we bring these out before our Christmas tree. But we're looking, especially, for the blessed Nativity.

Oh, what a wonderful true story of joy–to know all about Jesus, that heaven-sent boy. Shepherds of the field, wise men from afar–are part of the Nativity set, and the star.

Mary and Joseph and the baby on the hay–even the animals were "in on" Christmas Day. Surely, the human heart was meant to receive…the message of Christ's birth. It's so good to believe!

As for the children, each has such a tender heart. "Let them come" to Jesus before they depart, to one day leave your home to work or study in a distant place. Then they'll know the real meaning of Christmas and of God's amazing grace.

P. A. Oltrogge

"Then they brought little children to Him, that He might touch them; but the disciples rebuked those who brought them. But when Jesus saw it, He was greatly displeased and said to them, 'Let the little children come to Me, and do not forbid them; for of such is the kingdom of God. Assuredly, I say to you, whoever does not receive the kingdom of God as a little child will by no means enter it.'" Mark 10:13-15 NKJV

Come, as a little child, to our Savior

"…behold, I bring you good tidings of great joy which will be to all people. For there is born to you this day in the city of David a Savior, who is Christ the Lord." (From the account of Jesus' birth in Luke 2)

A Christmas Card Kept

A friend had sent me a Christmas card–an old-fashioned scene of a neighborhood with snow. It had just enough glitter to make the snow sparkle in what looked like a winter twilight's glow.

Cardinals rested on greenery; and a village church was prominent in the picture, which reminded of the true meaning of Christmas–written inside was a scripture.

"The Lord will perfect that which concerns me. Your mercy, oh Lord, endures forever." We are the works of His hands–Jesus promised to forsake us never.

We know that He will always stand by us–a great thought for all the year. The serenity of the village scene evoked assurance that, with God, there's nothing to fear.

Sometimes I may want to retreat…to a nostalgic village like that pictured on the card. But I can remember the Lord is perfecting things for me, anytime that a day may seem hard.

P. A. Oltrogge

"The Lord will perfect that which concerns me; Your mercy, oh Lord, endures forever; Do not forsake the works of Your hands."
Psalm 138:8 NKJV

"For we are His workmanship, created in Christ Jesus unto good works, which God hath before ordained that we should walk in them."
Ephesians 2:10 KJV

"Know that the Lord, He is God; It is He who has made us, and not we ourselves; We are His people, and the sheep of His pasture."
Psalm 100:3 NKJV

"…be content with such things as you have. For He Himself has said, 'I will never leave you nor forsake you.'" from Hebrews 13:5 NKJV

"But godliness with contentment is great gain." 1 Timothy 6:6 KJV

"I sought the Lord, and He answered me, and delivered me from all my fears." Psalm 34:4 NASB

Poinsettias for the Prince of Peace

At the Christmas season, with decorations inside and out,
the poinsettias reflect what it's all about.
Clean as the whiteness of a lamb or a dove—
the purity of ivory petals speaks of the Child sent from above.

Pink reflects cheer and the joy that was proclaimed
by the angels about the Christ child—Jesus, He's named.
Crimson red speaks of blood that was shed for mankind
by Jesus Christ upon the cross—our salvation defined.

The lives of those who receive Him gain a new lease
in finding faith for living through this Prince of Peace.
So, in seeing the poinsettias, rejoice for the reason
that His birth in Bethlehem is what gave us this season.

P. A. Oltrogge

"And, lo, the angel of the Lord came upon them, and the glory of the
Lord shone round about them: and they were sore afraid. And the angel
said unto them, 'Fear not: for behold, I bring you good tidings of great joy,
which shall be to all people. For unto you is born this day in the city of
David, a Saviour, which is Christ the Lord.'"
Luke 2:9-11 KJV

"But as many as received him, to them gave he power to become the sons
of God, even to them that believe on his name." John 1:12 KJV

Our Everliving Jesus

Jesus, the Son of God, was birthed by Mary and laid in a manger.
King Herod sought to kill Him, but He was kept from danger...
for His earthly father, Joseph, having been enlightened and driven,
by instructions in a dream that the angel of the Lord had given,
took the Child and His mother away to a distant Egyptian location.
And, there, the family stayed for a specified duration.

In later years, during Jesus' ministry, others opposed Him, too.
But no one could actually harm Him until His ministry days were through.
The devil himself confronted Jesus, with temptations to disband
from loyalty to the Godhead and to all that was divinely planned.
Jesus was obedient, however, to His Father throughout His days.
Then, even death, with its finality, couldn't hold Him—God be praised!

Today, some seek to downplay Jesus' divinity or worldwide fame,
or they deny acknowledging the Lordship of His name.
But His is a name that's above all names—an everlasting name,
a name through which we're made righteous, for He took all our blame.
And one day every knee shall bow, acknowledging all that's been said,
of Jesus Christ as Lord of all, who is surely the Church's head.

Some, who are doubtful, try to put Jesus completely out of thought,
abandoning the Christian truths that they were previously taught.
But His is a name which we should praise, and certainly not ignore,
for there IS no other God—Jesus said, "I am the Door."
How will we escape if we neglect so great a salvation,
which God has freely offered to all people of every nation?

It is through Jesus Christ that God has sought to bless us all.
He's the one and only Savior sent to redeem us from man's fall.
He's the Alpha and Omega, the beginning and the end...
and about whom the scriptures most assuredly were penned.

And, thankfully, we can bring to Jesus any problem, large or small.
He's "The Everlasting Father," on whom we're privileged to call.

P. A. Oltrogge

"For unto us a child is born, unto us a son is given: and the government shall be upon his shoulder: and his name shall be called Wonderful, Counsellor, The mighty God, The Everlasting Father, The Prince of Peace."
Isaiah 9:6 KJV

"Jesus said unto them, Verily, verily, I say unto you, Before Abraham was, I am." John 8:58 KJV

"Jesus said to him, 'I am the way, the truth, and the life. No one comes to the Father except through Me. If you had known Me, you would have known My Father also; and from now on you know Him and have seen Him.' Philip said to Him, 'Lord, show us the Father, and it is sufficient for us.' Jesus said to him, 'Have I been with you so long, and yet you have not known me, Philip? He who has seen Me has seen the Father; so how can you say, 'Show us the Father'?" John 14:6-9 NKJV

"I and My Father are one." John 10:30 NKJV

"For if the word spoken through angels proved unalterable, and every transgression and disobedience received a just penalty, how will we escape if we neglect so great a salvation? After it was at the first spoken through the Lord, it was confirmed to us by those who heard, God also testifying with them, both by signs and wonders and by various miracles and by gifts of the Holy Spirit according to His own will." Hebrews 2:2-4 NASB

"And He is the head of the body, the church: who is the beginning, the firstborn from the dead; that in all things he might have the preeminence."
Colossians 1:18 KJV

"And whatever you do in word or deed, do all in the name of the Lord Jesus, giving thanks to God the Father through Him." Colossians 3:17 NKJV

"...casting all your care upon Him, for He cares for you." 1 Peter 5:7 NKJV

The Depth of My Love

What do you think drove me from heaven above
down to this earth? It was the depth of my love.
Betrayed by a kiss, a symbol of such–
yet what drove me on was that I loved you so much.
When they led me away and gave me a shove,
what kept me going was the depth of my love.
They gave me a trial, but it was not just–
bitter to go through, but my heart said, "I must."
A crown of thorns pushed down with a glove,
it bruised my head to show the depth of my love.
The whipping I took for sin in your place,
I found strength to take because I saw your face.
I've loved you, I've called you–you are my dove,
for whom I laid down my life with the depth of my love.
The weight of the cross became hard to bear–
I staggered but made it to Calvary there.
On those merciless beams, my hands and feet were nailed down.
Next, I was put on display to be mocked throughout town.
Then came the time of greatest agony and despair,
when I felt forsaken but still kept my care
for all of mankind and, yes, just for you.
For your welfare and soul, I had made it through.
So what kept me going when push came to shove?
From your "down to earth" God, it was the depth of my love.
Though your sins be as scarlet, they'll be white as snow.
They're forgiven and forgotten and now you can grow
in the knowledge and wisdom that comes from above,
and my Word will remind you of the depth of my love.

P. A. Oltrogge

"As the Father loved Me, I also have loved you; abide in My love. If you keep My commandments, you will abide in My love, just as I have kept My Father's commandments and abide in His love." John 15:9-10 NKJV

Printed in the United States
By Bookmasters